The Magic of Chelsea

2025

A Flower Show Like No Other

Christine Thompson-Wells

Chelsea brings people together...

If you purchase this book without its cover, it may be stolen.

Neither the publisher nor the author is under any obligation to provide professional services in any way, legal, health, or in any form that is related to this book, its contents, advice, or otherwise.

The law and practices vary from country to country and state to state.

If legal or professional information is required, the purchaser or reader should seek it privately, in a manner best suited to their particular needs and circumstances.

The author and publisher expressly disclaim any liability that may be incurred as a result of the information contained in this book.

All rights reserved. No part of this book, including the interior design, images, cover design, diagrams, or any intellectual property (IP), icons and photographs, may be reproduced or transmitted in any form by any means (electronic, photocopying, recording or otherwise) without the prior permission of the publisher. ©

Copyright© 2025 MSI Australia

All rights reserved.

ISBN: 978-1-7642897-0-2

Published by How2Books
Under license from MSI Ltd, Australia
Company Registration No: 96963518255
NSW, Australia

See our website: www.how2books.com.au
Or contact by email: sales@how2books.com.au

Covers and Copyright owned by MSI, Australia

MSI acknowledges the author and images, text and photographs used in this book.

10% of each book's sale helps support Diabetes Type One and Cancer Research.

The Magic of Moments – Peony Roses...

Moments quickly fade and go, for if not captured, the valuable time spent will only be wasted, and there will be a time to lament –

not for a moment must time be forgotten...

Life is for living, and even when times are rough and sadness creeps in,

there are times for regrets and times for cheer, but each is filled with moments, and one must adhere...

The moments of the Chelsea Flower Show each year become memories, and from those memories we learn and grow...

Only for the next time, our thoughts wander, as many moments will linger as memories considered:

what a splendid time we had at Chelsea 2025...

With flowers as crystals gleaming on such a splendid day, the moments are cherished, and no one can deny that the exhibits of all were exceeded by none.

It is the moment we capture from the flowers we see, more than can be imagined from the seeds they sew, and the magnificence seen is beyond anything we know...!

From time to time, a moment is missed, and yet, we linger and still want to know, how did this magnificent creation in its glory and the beauty to show...?

The moment of seeing the peony rose this year was beyond anything we've seen.

Is it a perfumery or a jewel of nature created?

It is there, fragrant and perfumed, so the bumble bees gather too many to count...

They feverishly hover, so much pollen to gather, and yet so many people are there, all wanting to see...

The bumble bees buzz from bloom to bloom, the people look on at such magnificence seen, is this for real, or is it a dream…?

The magic of Chelsea has more to unfold from year to year, a different dream will reveal…

The moments make the memories we have, so count each one, for it might be just that - it connects you to your moonbeam, and then to your dream…

Welcome to The Magic of Chelsea 2025…

On our arrival at Heathrow Airport, we collect our pre-ordered rental car. It's always a challenge to know which type of vehicle we'll be travelling around the South of England in each year. Usually, it's a pleasant surprise, and this year our rental company did itself proud in issuing us with a new car that was royal blue, so the visit started well.

Leaving our daughter's home early, just as the sun was rising, was magnificent. Though the land was dry, the newly iridescent greens of the tree leaves were on show. The blue sky, birds chirping in the early morning air, made the day set to be magnificent, and it was set to be a superb day.

On the drive into London, my husband and I chatted; we spoke about everything and nothing all at the same time. Arriving at the parking lot and parking the car, we walked a short distance to the show entrance gates, which were just one of the pleasures of the day.

The atmosphere, as usual, was electric. People didn't have time to be miserable; it was Show Day and a day to be enjoyed by thousands of people, some travelling, like ourselves, from faraway places.

The weather was superb, with the freshness and perfume of the flowers lingering in every breath taken. The flowers on display had gems of dew and a sharpness of colour, crystals of purity within the petals, and a magnificence to behold.

The foliage of the plants was so tender yet firm; they, too, had their mastery in the displays they created.

The Chelsea Flower Show 2025 was superb. From flowers and plants, to sculpture and individual displays of produce from farms and villages, some from Europe, were all there in the glorious early morning sunshine of the spring day of 2025.

Christine

Christine Thompson-Wells
Author of Many Books

A Wonderful 2025...
Chelsea Flower Show

Content   Page

Chelsea brings people together…	
The magic of the moments – Peony roses - Poem	
Welcome to the Magic of Chelsea – an excellent 2025 - flower show	
Amazing Chelsea, 2025, roses	1
Vegetable Surprises	4
Mixed Iris blooms	6
The Iris Flower – Poem	8
The beautiful Iris flower	9
Alstroemeria flowers	10
Red and white Azaleas	11
GLASS – The magic of the medium	12
Creative expression	14
Magnificent Delphinium	15
Tropical plants and flowers – Antigua and Barbuda	16
Stunning Acer trees	20
Bonsai	21
Allium flowers	23
Fantastic water features	25
Continuing with water features	26
Garden delights – unique water features	27
Happy garden features	28
Flourishing Floristry and Floral Art	29
Wild meadows could not give more…	30
Beautiful	31
Looking at the three-dimensional design	32
A slightly different angle	33
Reaching for the stars	34
Different approaches give different outcomes	35
Remarkable red	36
Amazing design	37
The beauty of the curve	38
The Veil	39
A time to take notice	40
Healthy plants are becoming suffocated by commercial debris and rubbish	41
Creative circular shapes	42
Creative circles and design	43
Cattley orchids	44
Fascinating Phalaenopsis	46
Bronze expression – Susan Long	47
Hippeastrum	49
A splendid display	50
Different foliage	51
Mushrooms	52

The Little Flower Hut	54
Peony roses	55
The beauty continues	
Grasses	58
My Sweet Pea Story	59
Perfect stone	60
The sculpture of stone – Poem	61
Begonias in abundance	62
Stoned fruit, orb water features and containers	63
Plant biometrics	64
Plant Heritage UK	65
Flora of South Africa	66
Taking the Chelsea guests into the story	67
The female face	68
Succulents	69
Old-fashioned delight	70
Corten chain expression & solid-welded metal – creating art	71
When a creative mind is allowed to have fun	72
Dibley's Colour	73
Agapanthus flowers	74
Farewell Flowers	75
The Journey – Poem	77
Disbud chrysanthemums	78
A magnificent bloom	79
Marble & stone carvings	81
Perfect in white	82
Cacti & succulents	83
Hosta plants	84
Tulips	85
The Seed of Obsession	87
Small gardens for unique spaces	89
Oriental lilies	94
Clematis wonder	95
The art of seeing	97
Wild & free – all created from found wood	98
Arisaema Sikokianum	100
Jacques Amand	101
Feature a circle	103
Tonal value & space	104
Different outside gardens – British Red Cross Garden	105
Save for a rainy day, Garden	106
The Avanade Intelligent Garden	107
Children with Cancer – 'A Place to Be'	108
The 'O' shape	109
Spectacular Zantedeschi – plants & more	110
Pretty as paint	111
The Flowers We See Today – Poem	112

Nature's offering & so much more	113
Looming threat – the Colorado Beetle	114
The weather was lovely.	115
Inspiration from an empty space – Catkin Blooms Winkleigh, Devon, United Kingdom	116
My words to you	119
Life Skills Education Association	120
Other books available	121

Chelsea, 2025 – Roses

As we wander into the Great Pavilion each year, the perfume of the roses wafts through the air, introducing themselves. The scent is like a signpost heralding, *'We are here, don't miss us, we have a great display this year.'*

The magical flower displays at Chelsea 2025 were beyond speech and such a joy to experience.

From traditional to new varieties, each was a splendid display, as evident in these photographs. Floribunda and single, beautiful specimens all have their story to tell.

The rose is believed to have originated in Asia Minor, which is today's modern Turkey. First

identified in approximately 250 BCE, roses have spread across the world, with many single varieties now cultivated in parts of Africa for the international flower market.

The Magic of Chelsea 2025

From the singular beauty of unfurling petals to the mass explosion cascading colours of different shapes and sizes, all could be seen at this year's show.

Roses have many uses beyond their beauty. They are used in medicinal products, perfumes, and for festive and celebratory cake decorations.

Of course, we cannot deny our emotional attachment to roses. We use this flower to let another person know that we care and that we are thinking of them. There is also the unspoken word of love when given to another person.

And so it is; this flower, loved by many generations, still holds its status as it displays its beauty in this year's show.

The yellow floribunda seen below was exceptional, not only in its shape and the formation of its petals and colour, but it has an exquisite perfume that might be a sprinkle of pleasure given from a passing angel!

While we wander the show, gasp, and take so many photographs for this book, it's easy to forget that the pictures must be continually taken; otherwise, we will run out of time. This perfect pink rose bud opposite stopped me in my tracks. It was a piece of nature's sculpture, and it was a pleasure to see.

Roses can catch us by surprise; we may be out on a casual walk, alone on a winter's day, and a single rose blooms in a garden – you stop, look, and marvel at this incredible pleasure that is just yours for the moment, and a moment shared…

The Magic of Chelsea 2025

Vegetable Surprises

A show stopper for sure. This remarkable stand stood alone in *'difference.'*

With so many ultra-processed and processed foods, as well as artificial colours, being added to soft drinks, all of which are available on supermarket shelves, we need more innovative displays like this. Displays that show the public the goodness, variety, and colour of freshly grown vegetables and fruit.

Below, the richness of colour and the many reds from the stems of the rhubarb to the bunch of red tomatoes, from red to orange of the nasturtiums of abundance and in their orange tones to the left of the photograph.

Then to purples, including the cauliflowers, purple zucchini, and various tonal greens.

4

From the heart of the purple cabbage, on the previous page, the fusion of different greens straddled through the display and composition. The complete display was circular, which made it easy for Chelsea spectators to walk around, ponder, and enjoy the display.

The fascination of colour, texture, and shape is all brought about by the careful placement of each element, considering all design fundamental concepts used in creative work.

The smoky hue of different greens also had a role in the display and elements of this design.

When children are made aware that colour is also a part of the food they eat, they will develop a different appreciation for the 'real' value and quality of the food available to them.

The Magic of Chelsea 2025

Mixed Iris Blooms

Goodness, these iris blooms must be a gift from the heavenly spheres sent to us mortals to enjoy and take a moment to linger and absorb the pleasure of such beauty.

This year's display of irises was beyond the words written in this book.

Their magnificence was anything beyond anything I have seen from the iris producers, but here they are, on the pages before you, a magical gift for us all to see.

The blending of rich, red, velvety colours and textures, regent golds, all cascading from their leaves and the displays on show.

It is not surprising that the kings of France have used the fleur-de-lis as an emblem identifying the three petals as faith, wisdom and valour.

Indeed, the fleur-de-lis is still seen in many royal decorations today, so the shape is not outdated or old-fashioned.

The mastery of combining two intense colours, purple and gold, and the infusion of white on the outer petals, showcases the mastery of nature and its persistence in giving us the 'WOW' factor in the beauty this flower displays.

Somehow, it's difficult not to imagine that a fairy or ballerina will eventually emerge from this beautiful flower...!

On the right, the crimson of the petals and the transition to the gold of the beards and then to the falls or outer petals, which show the gentle softness of colour. All of the iris flowers were magical in their displays.

Such contrasts in colours, with fragrance to match, each a perfect example of what nature can produce...

As a child, I remember the purple-bearded iris blooming in discarded soil dumps and along country lanes in England. They would grow each year and reveal their splendour. At that time, I never thought I would feel such wonder for such a perfect flower...!

The Iris Flower

Chelsea, 2025 was a fabulous show – the iris display with colour of vibrance, and for all to see...

From purples to whites and crinkle-cut edges, to yellows to pinks and with little time to think...

The iris flowers, as usual, wanted to speak, 'Look at us...' Have you ever seen such beauty all in one place..?

And this was all happening while we looked at their space...

Not a blemish was to be seen, and all were majestic for the viewers that day, for their beauty time is of the essence and petals will fade...

From the beauty to translucent, they no longer reveal their magnificence and no longer do they fill....

A space they once had, and the beauty displayed is just for a short moment, and all that is left is how we all feel...

For generations before us, they once would confirm, the majestic this bloom and to again, their hearts they would yearn...

With petals as perfect as angel's gossamer wings, nothing quite like it can humans produce, and yet that is the wonder of which we confirm...

These flowers have been a part of our planet's perception
And to this glory we have this connection...

Life is too short for wars to persist
like the iris, our souls are such that make living hard to resist...

It is the blooms of the flower that bring solace to us, and an anchor in time that makes us aware,

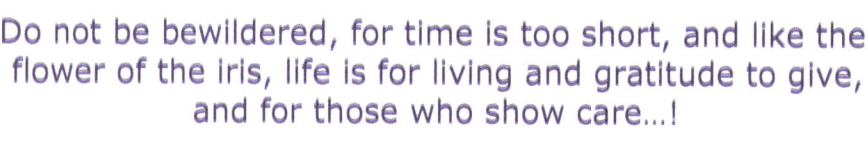

Do not be bewildered, for time is too short, and like the flower of the iris, life is for living and gratitude to give, and for those who show care...!

The Magic of Chelsea 2025

The Beautiful Iris Flower

Alstroemeria Flowers

Seeing alstroemeria flowers in such abundance, displayed in tall urns at Chelsea this year, was a delight.

When I was undergoing floristry training in the 1960s, the flowers were not as strong or vibrant in colour as they are today. When we look deeply into the golden florets opposite, there is strength in the delight they show; they are proud specimens, taking pleasure in the attention they receive from the Chelsea crowds.

Alstroemeria, also known as Peruvian lilies, originates from South America. They were discovered in the 17th century by the Swedish botanist, Baron Claus von Alstromer. He documented their uniqueness and was fascinated by the trumpet shape of the flower head.

Now, in the 2020s, these flowers are widely used in garden beds for vivid displays, and by the cut flower industry and by florists in various flower arrangements. Whether used in combination with other flowers or as a solo appearance, they are a flower that makes a significant presence in grand displays.

Red & White Azaleas

This display of azaleas was different, as there are many suspicions in our thinking about pairing red and white flowers; however, such combinations can be eye-catching and captivating.

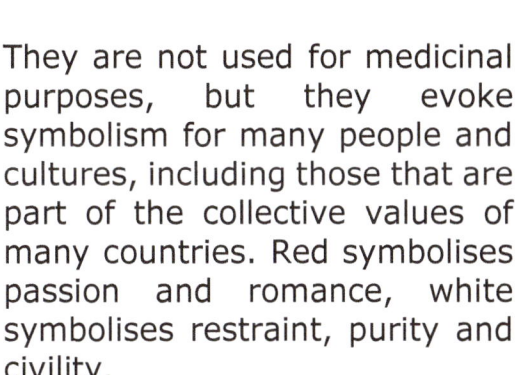

The azalea, originally from the rhododendron family, was initially found in Asia, parts of Europe, including China, and North America.

They are not used for medicinal purposes, but they evoke symbolism for many people and cultures, including those that are part of the collective values of many countries. Red symbolises passion and romance, white symbolises restraint, purity and civility.

They do give a beautiful display in gardens and are always a pleasure to see, especially as captured in these photographs.

The vividness of the colour, the perfection of the flower, and the gentle, heavenly perfume softly filling the air were yet another beautiful memory to cherish in our day.

The Magic of Chelsea 2025

GLASS – The Magic of the Medium

This translucent material has been used since ancient times, and even now, the creations artists produce are as captivating as they were in the days of our ancestors.

Glass is one of the oldest functional materials used in building, dating back more than 4,000 years.

Initially, glass was found on the beaches, and through the sun's heat, many glass-like shapes were transformed from sand into

glass crystals, forming different forms; this marked the beginning of human identification of the material.

So, glass is made from silica, or sand, through high-temperature processes. It is heated and then shaped into various objects, including windows and functional bowls used in our homes. Here, in these photographs, you can see the artistry of the material in full splendour.

From the mind of the artist, Carrie Anne Funnell, to the glass shapes seen in these creations, they are all part of the malleability of glass.

Carrie Anne and I briefly spoke about the purity of glass, the purity of colour, and the creativity that can be imagined and then created through heat and creative ability. When combining glass with a metal, such as stainless steel, the togetherness becomes a magical combination of imaginative fun.

From swirls of white interchanged with deep magenta and the formation

of shapes within the pattern, the creative force always has energy, and this is possibly part of the magic the artist creates for us to see…

Opposite, discs of glass are attached to a metal archway, allowing the sun's light to reflect in separate pieces of glass.

Due to the looseness of each disc, they would move independently. This allowed different elements, colours, and light to be seen.

Creative Expression

Freedom of expression has been an integral part of individual personality since humans began painting images in caves, over 60,000 years ago.

Other images of the human body have been carved into rocks, providing us with messages dating back to at least 27,000 years ago or longer.

Today, we find creative expression from the use of papier-mache in the

construction of the face, and the dyed grasses in the headdress!

From the Ban the Bomb image of the sixties, to the blackened lips of 'punk rockers', all could be seen in this fantastic piece of artistry within floristry design.

Precision in the creative shape of the face draws the eye to the extremities of the design, where a beautiful flower display of green anthuriums and purple alliums is showcased.

Magnificent Delphiniums

Delphiniums are striking in their colours and a tremendous asset in large flower design displays.

They originally came from the mountainous areas of Northern Europe and Africa.

Though spectacular in their appearance, they are toxic, like many plants, to humans and animals, so care should be taken when handling them. I have used thousands of delphiniums in large flower arrangements, but I'm cautious when arranging flowers and having lunch at the same time. Always wash your hands before you eat…

I have made wired headdresses from single flower florets. Each floret must be wired onto silver wire, which is then attached to an already pre-made, wired, and shaped frame. Wired delphinium florets will last about six hours, usually the time of a complete wedding and the ceremony.

Of course, only a **Gold** Award is sufficient for such a magnificent display…

Tropical Flowers & Plants – Antigua & Barbuda

And, the plants and displays of 2025 just kept on giving... The delight of every display was just that - incredible pleasure to see, admire, and have the privilege of travelling the distances we did to take the photographs, and to have the ability to bring these beautiful images together in this book.

Not only were the exhibits a delight, but the creativity of the flower arrangers in all the magnificent displays must also be highly commended. It takes years of creating and learning to master any floral design.

The pink ginger lily flowers from Antigua and Barbuda are a stunning arrangement, thoughtfully designed and crafted for this year's show.

Opposite, tropical pink leaves, clusters of what resembled pink bananas and cascading green heliconia flowers. When such colours are combined, they create a striking and unique configuration for flower arranging.

The pink ginger lily plant from Antigua & Barbuda is just one magnificent arrangement carefully thought about and constructed at this year's show.

Opposite, tropical pink leaves, clusters of what resembled pink bananas and cascading green heliconia flowers. When such colours are combined, they create a striking and unique configuration for flower arranging.

From different perspectives, the stand presents distinct views of various tropical flowers and their displays.

As can be seen in the opposite photograph, anthurium flowers are a prominent feature of the display.

In my varied career as a teacher and having trained as a florist before going to university, I counselled and taught young male offenders in the prison system in the United Kingdom. Some young males were very difficult to become motivated until one day, I announced that 'we are all going to do some painting.' The motivation was slow until I started drawing and then painting the finished drawing of an anthurium flower.

The transformation by these young people was miraculous and an absolute pleasure to see.

Creating and painting the anthurium flowers took some weeks, but eventually, every young male in the program had an anthurium flower painting in his cell. That shows you the power, communication and consideration have…!

The beautiful anthurium flower comes in many different colours, including white to soft pink and deep maroon reds, all of which are a delight to arrange.

In the opposite photograph, the white anthuriums contrast strongly with the dark green of the elongated leaves, providing a smooth transition to the vibrancy of the colours seen on the stand.

The backdrop of the mud and stone-built castle was also a nice addition to what was a very pleasing and energetic display of colour and formation of different flowers, foliage and fresh ideas.

From the coolness of white and the contrasting green, we see in the photograph opposite a vibrant splash of colour, ranging from pinks to sharply contrasting greens, and then the deep maroon of tropical leaves. All add to a complex pattern of interwoven colour and energy.

In this next photograph, orchids of vivid orange and burning red cascade down the design, with ginger flowers taking a stand, leaping skyward, and then the deep red foliage of the cordyline plant anchors the arrangement, providing a solid foundation for the design.

The red and orange hues of the heliconia flower sweep upwards, drawing our eyes to the iridescent green ferns that interrupt our vision through their soft, gentle fronds, whispering in the breeze that fills the open doors of the Great Pavilion.

Part of the feature of this display was the use of beautiful Queen Conch cut sea shells and pink sand, giving the impression that all people are welcome…

It is the continuous round shape of the shells used to create a pattern of interest and difference that is so enthralling about the whole presentation of the display, lovely and a privilege to see and experience.

Stunning Acer Trees

The Acer is often referred to as a maple tree, and that is correct. They have an interesting lineage dating back approximately 100 to 120 million years.

The earliest known fossil was found in Alaska. From that time, they spread across Northern Europe and into China.

The original leaf shape had just three lobes and was very different from the leaf shape we know today.

They are a beautiful tree, giving off a splendid backdrop to many gardens. Not only is the tree a great feature, but the array of colours seen in autumn cannot be beaten with eye-catching and dramatic displays of colour from yellows, through to burnt oranges and then the subtle soft brown tones of the season.

Bonsai

Many people become mesmerised by the shapes and perfection of the Bonsai trees. This year, we were treated to exceptional displays, and we can only showcase a few in this book.

From expertly shaped azalea trees to the magnificent fir, all were on display this year.

Gnarled wood adds to the splendour of the exhibits, some dating back a hundred years or more.

Creating intriguing visual stopping points within the growth of these ornamental displays gives us time to pause and appreciate the creative insight into how the tree has been shaped over many years.

Texture and colour play a creative role in the presentation of these displays. From continuous care to an excellent presentation, it all takes dedication and love to execute.

With so many Bonsai on display this year, it was rewarding to see how many different trees can be grown this way.

The original art of Bonsai goes back to the sixth century in China; from there, the art then travelled to Japan.

It was the imperial and embassy officials, as well as Buddhist students from Japan, who further developed this art form during their stays in China and upon their return to Japan. The word Bonsai means: contained in a container.

The art form closely resembles the shape of a fully matured tree growing naturally in nature.

Allium Flowers

If you are a flower arranger, then you will possibly love to work with long-stemmed allium flowers...

They make a spectacular display for modern or massed flower arrangements.

ALL WHITE AND A TREAT...

I love white flowers, either in the garden or in all-white flower arrangements.

White and green combinations can give a feeling of elegance and sophistication to any room; it doesn't have to be a wedding to use such colours in today's world of design.

The perfect accompaniment for florists and flower arrangers, tall alliums allow floral designs to reach elegance and dignity in height, grandeur, and majesty. They are ideal for extensive display work in churches, grand halls, weddings, and at flower shows.

Fantastic Water Features

Water features made from the ancient art of terracotta clay looked fantastic.

Terracotta, as we know, is an ancient building material that is still widely used today. We purchase terracotta oven cookware and plant pots, all of which are crafted from terracotta. It is a natural and environmentally friendly product that can be used repeatedly.

In these photographs, there is an extensive use of this ancient building product. With the increasing emphasis on making our homes environmentally friendly, it's great to see these indoor and outdoor water features.

The plantings can go from water grasses and plants to the iconic water lily.

Not only are water features environmentally friendly, but they are also ideal for reducing stress, which can help lower blood pressure. They support relaxation of the mind, and the gentle movement of water enhances our visual pleasure.

Continuing with Water Features

It is not only the people of the 21st Century who enjoy water features; water has been a feature throughout human history. The Romans, who could afford it, would have fountains built into garden features; the Japanese have water as a feature and as a protector as part of their garden features.

Another of the stands at this year's Chelsea offered a new perspective on the water feature, which would make a welcome attribute to the smaller townhouse gardens, increasingly featured in newer homes. Water features made from bronze in the shape of trees were stunning, and the gentle trickle of water was peaceful to hear on such a busy show day.

From the flowing water from trees to the gentle droplets from the open flowers.

Each separate creation, whether large or small, would make a lovely addition to any garden, regardless of its size.

Garden Delights – Unique Water Features…

Glass and bronze flowers make this an exceptional display, and what a perfect combination of ancient materials.

The tree leaves represent the maple tree in midsummer. At the same time, the perfect shape of the glass lilies shows us how these majestic materials have been used throughout many ages and civilisations.

The Magic of Chelsea 2025

Happy Garden Features

At first glance, something makes you smile; you instantly know that what you are seeing makes you happy, and this is the immediate effect of seeing these very different garden features and furniture.

From large lemons to ornate and beautiful cherries, as seen in the photograph below.

Then, in the photograph above, there is this very cheeky citrus green garden seat, or perhaps, a seat on a balcony…! The possibilities are endless when you take the time to consider how a different feel can be achieved in any outside setting through the addition of one or two other pieces of furniture; there is no limit to the fun that can be created.

Flourishing Floristry & Floral Art

A hand-tied bunch in perfect placement won **GOLD** in this category of Floral Art. The perfection and creativity of the workmanship were outstanding and such a pleasure to see. To hold so many flowers in the hand while arranging them would have taken control and stamina to achieve the final result, as seen in these two photographs.

Wild Meadows Could Not Give More…

Another **GOLD** for the combination of three arrangements to form one display. Wildflowers, moss, and lichen-covered wood, along with the gentle placement of delicate wildflowers, make this an exceptional piece of floristry work.

The Magic of Chelsea 2025

Beautiful...

Creativity abounds in this forward-thinking design, as evidenced by the placement of flowers, dried reeds, and grasses.

The swish of the curves from the larger to the smaller keeps your eyes moving, taking in the soft and gently coloured flowers and the placements made. Pinks, pale blue, deeper blue and soft beige dried whisps of palm fronds add to the interest created in the lower arrangement.

The rope edging gives a solid edge to the design, and yet we all know that rope can be moved very easily…

It was an absolute joy to experience and see the work committed to this and many other displays at this year's show.

Another design wins **GOLD.**

Looking at the Three-Dimensional Aspect of the Design...

From what has been previously described, it is now easier to see the entire three-dimensional aspect of this well-crafted floral design. This is a **GOLD-**winning masterpiece.

A Slightly Different Angle...

Fascinating, different, and so impressive. This design combines all the elements of floral art and floristry, creating a visual delight that showcases how various design elements can work together to create design magic.

Tight catkin branches have been held and shaped into a semi-arc to create this captivating arrangement, from the soft fronds of the sweeping white feathers above to the anchor provided by pure white anemones at the base.

It features a blend of different elements, colours, and textures that make it a fascinating study.

Reaching for the Stars...

This tall and elegant arrangement shows the ease of placement, movement, rhythm, and texture.

From the wispy placements of light-green foliage to the visual resting places of the lilies. The intermingling of apricot small lantern shapes, possibly a small pepper, through to the Moluccella laevis or Bells of Ireland green stems, and then sweeping your eyes upwards with strength, are the apricot Foxglove flowers.

The black shape of a hat or circle gives the overall appearance of a Spanish-themed design.

For several reasons, this remarkable design is worthy of mention in this book this year.

Different Approaches Give Different Outcomes

It wins **GOLD.** It's very different in the materials used in the construction of the design, and yet, it is the difference that is so appealing.

From bleached, dried grasses wisping like an umbrella over the design and the speckles of silver hanging loosely in the air, all contribute to this distinctive design.

Punching their way through the creation are the solid balls of pink and purple flowers, with a

profusion of oranges exploding and coming forward, an air of wanting to be noticed.

Subtle blues meander from the base of the design, up and through the focal area and then slowly fade into the distance. It is the difference that draws the connection by the spectators to each design seen at this year's show.

The Magic of Chelsea 2025

Remarkable Red

Again, red is used in the massed arrangement. The colour is indeed striking and gives a dramatic contrast to the white and green foliage used.

When a country uses their flag colour in the flowers it uses, it shows commitment, a sense of ownership, and a sense of pride in its home.

With careful placement, the flowers tell the story. Telling a story was indeed part of this year's theme, as evident in the flower arrangements on display.

The red Anthuriums in the opposite photograph are superb examples of this excellent exotic flower.

Traditional fabric supports the overall theme, coming to life and again giving the impression of a sense of belonging.

We have another **GOLD** for this exhibit, and it is well-deserved.

The Magic of Chelsea 2025

Amazing Designs

Expressive creations come about through subtle messaging. In this beautiful creation, the artist takes their idea from a seed to a seedling, and then draws inspiration for growth and life from the seedling's emergence from the ground into the light and life.

From the traditional Tao Chinese philosophy, this design exemplifies the

togetherness of nature. It reminds us that, from an enormous oak tree to a tiny grass seed, it is the infinite energy of life that sustains existence. It is the journey of all life forms and the determination to survive that allows them to exist.

The white shell base is made from various fabrics commonly used in traditional lantern-making.

This design is a remarkable, thought-provoking exhibit which stops you in your tracks and makes you think...
'Seed' Created by Guan Guan Art Studio.

The Beauty of the Curve...

During my training as a florist, a teacher told me, '*A curve is a deviation of a line...*' I have never forgotten that. Additionally, while studying for my teaching degree at the University of Canberra, I needed to complete two units unrelated to teaching. I chose to attend the Canberra School of Art, which I thoroughly enjoyed. Over that time, I studied Twentieth Century Art History and Sculpture. Again, I heard a lecturer say, '*A curve is a deviation of a line...*'

How great teachers think alike, even though they are worlds apart...! 'Moon in Bloom,' created by Kathryn Cronin, is a masterful execution of the curved line and a delightful exhibit.

The Veil

'Through the Veil.' There are many stories and philosophies expressed through floristry and flower arranging.

Before I went on to university, and while training as a florist, a constant question was always on my mind: 'Why do people buy flowers?' This was the exact question that eventually sent me to university. And the answer being: 'Because they have an emotional need to express their feelings, either to themselves or to another person...'

In this design, the floral artist pays tribute to her grandfather, who originally comes from India. The design is inspired by sehra bandi, a traditional headdress worn on the groom's head before he departs his home to meet his bride. It reflects the florist's thoughts of her grandfather and his struggle for respect in his new country, England, which has inspired this story told through an original arrangement of light-blue delphinium, antique roses, and champagne-coloured Lisianthus.

The Magic of Chelsea 2025

A Time to Take Notice...

Many young artists from various expressive genres are creating expressions and thoughts through mediums such as flowers, dried materials, and found or handmade objects. The upper part of the design depicts healthy plants and trees growing, while the lower part shows the root systems of each.

In this expression of creativity, artists Wagner Kreusch and Frida Kim draw on the dualities of living organisms, specifically the dualities of plants and the functioning of the human body.

The message conveyed connects the living systems of both plants and humans as a single, functioning organism.

HEALTHY PLANTS ARE BEING SUFFOCATED BY COMMERCIAL DEBRIS AND RUBBISH

PLANT SUFFOCATION, PESTICIDE DAMAGE, IMPORTED PARASITES, COMMERCIAL POLLUTANTS, SOIL EROSION AND DAMAGE

Young people, including many older artists, are concerned about commercial pesticides, mineral waste from mining, and other contaminants that are polluting the environments of inland waterways, land, sea, and air.

From industrial waste to junk littered on highways, all contribute to the degradation of the natural habitat of some rare plants, while neglecting to understand the needs of native animals, including birds and, of course, the bees that are essential for human survival.

Creative Circular Shapes...

A creative story of circular shapes, intertwined with willow decorated with moss and possibly lichen. The story shows a vibrancy of movement, colour and design. Respect for the elements of space and time reveals the diverse aspects of the flowers and foliage used.

Moving from pinks to lilacs, different greens in the foliage each followed the circular movements of the container and shapes used.

Creative minds work hard to bring their messages and visions to life in the floral displays showcased at this year's show.

With such movement and rhythm, it feels as though we are ready for a party…!

When floral artists are allowed to express their creativity in arranging flowers, the world becomes a veritable place of enjoyment, fun, and togetherness.

The Magic of Chelsea 2025

Creative Circles & Design...

Cattleya Orchids

An incredible display of Cattleya orchids was on display this year. As can be seen at a glance, the colours are vibrant and exciting, ranging from bright sunshine yellows to mellow creams; each has its distinct mark on the lip and its own character.

Cattleya orchids originated from Central and South America. Cattleya's come in varied sizes, mainly large, but are sometimes seen in smaller types.

Many produce a soft, delightful perfume. Cattleya orchids were commonly featured in wedding bouquets in the 1960s and 1970s. However, they are not as popular at present; like all stunning flowers, they will likely regain popularity as the choice flower for many brides.

As a decorative asset in the 1920s, many ladies would wear a corsage made of a single cattleya bloom, accompanied by a small ribbon bow and a maidenhair fern.

Stop for a moment, linger and take a moment to soak up the beauty of these magnificent creations of nature and the universe.

Orchids are not only a delight to look at, but the love of the orchid flower is now affecting our younger generations; they, too, are becoming captivated.

Orchids are not just ornamental beauties; they also have practical applications.

In traditional Chinese medicine, orchids are utilised for various medicinal purposes. Dried dendrobium is used as tea and is thought to help treat cancer, strengthen the immune system and improve eyesight.[1]

The vanilla orchid produces the vanilla bean and is one of the world's most popular flavours.

Orchids are one of the world's most endangered plant species; they require proper planting and soil conditions, as well as adequate watering and nutrition.

The exotic blooms seen here were originally from many and varied worldwide locations.

---

[1] Always check with your health provider before ingesting any medicinal products.

Fascinating Phalaenopsis

During my time as a working florist and before I became a writer, our florist shops would specialise in creative wedding work. To date, over the course of many years, I have created more than 5,000 wedding bouquets, and many of these would include the beautiful white Phalaenopsis orchids. It was a pleasure to see them so beautifully displayed at this year's Chelsea Flower Show.

A truly exotic and wonderful flower that exudes a great deal in terms of shape, texture, and expression.

Often seen in film and television production, creating an atmosphere of opulence, richness, and luxury, this flower says it all.

Not only is the flower long-lasting, but the distinct sharpness and contrast between the white of the flower and the rich green of the foliage make it suitable for display, and the combination makes a statement that is hard to resist in terms of visual impact.

The Magic of Chelsea 2025

Bronze Expression – Susan Long

Every time I see the work of Susan Long, I have to stop, look and stop myself from having a conversation with every one of her bronze statues.

From the three young women having a female conversation while they sit on a bench, and it may be a park bench, we don't know… Or it may be a bench at the end of the garden…!

To give to the onlooker the feeling that they, too, are part of the conversation takes our mind to another level.

Then there are the dancing nymphs, possibly seen on a dark but starry night. My imagination runs wild with how I would communicate with such mastery of bronze.

To have just one beautiful piece of this outstanding work in our garden in Australia would indeed be an accomplishment.

However, for now, I will revel in the beautiful photographs of Susan's work.

The Magic of Chelsea 2025

From the gentle lines of the woman's hat opposite, the flowing line is then picked up in the base of the young girl dancing. The flowing ruffles in the petticoat as she moves are all part of the enchantment of Susan's bronze creations.

The bronze creations evoke emotion from the viewer, creating a sense of connection and a desire to be part of the story being told.

From the feeling of connection, to the experience of wanting to join the young woman opposite as she strolls on her country walk, possibly in the late afternoon.

Then we look at the enchanting connection between the animal of a loving horse and the tiny figure of a young girl, almost whispering her secrets to the animal. She can tell her friend because she knows it will not be said to anyone else.

And so it is, the art of storytelling is in the formation of this ancient metal. Many civilisations have used bronze in casting, dating back to around 2,500 BCE, and we still see the wonders of creation when our talented artists produce such splendid and unique art forms.

The Magic of Chelsea 2025

Hippeastrum

From single blooms to mass showings, the hippeastrum shows us all just how special they can be when featured as a unique and beautiful flower.

From fiery reds to pinks and lovely whites, this flower has it all, colour, shape, texture and visual movement.

The plant has been cultivated to include a variety of petal shapes, which can be stunning to see. The range of colour is also varied from stark white to cream and an amazing iridescent green with an inner star-marking that gives the flower a uniqueness not seen in any other flowers. The Hippeastrum is also sometimes referred to as the Amaryllis lily. It is a native plant to the tropical regions of the Americas, including Mexico, Argentina and the Caribbean.

For a festive touch at Christmas time, place three to four plants in a large basket with straw securing the pots, and add a bow of a similar colour on the handle or rest it on a pot, thus creating a warm welcome in the hallway for any visitors at that time of year.

The Magic of Chelsea 2025

A Splendid Display...

Different Foliage

One of the exercises I was given when I was training in floristry, and I have since passed this exercise on to my students, and this is it: *'When you go for a walk, look at the trees, and see how much black you can see...'*

It is an excellent exercise for sharpening up your visual perception. It allows you to awaken your inner senses to colour, movement, and this visual awareness plays a key role in all forms of art.

In the photograph below, the pale candles of the spruce tree are highlighted by shadow, adding depth to the plant's blackness.

The Magic of Chelsea 2025

Mushrooms...

Mushrooms are fun to grow and to see the different shapes and colours emerging from other producers.

Opposite, the yellow oyster mushroom takes pride of place and is just one of the stand's features.

From the humble native mushroom to these extraordinary, creative, edible mushrooms of many colours and shapes.

The lower left exhibit resembles the chocolate seen on top of a cake or an ice cream tub. But it is a mushroom...!

Below is part of the display of the mushroom exhibit.

From the image of fingers or tentacles of a sea creature or a creature living in the depths of a dark and lonely forest... This mushroom would possibly scare you to death if you saw it in the middle of the night...!

Surprisingly, mushrooms have been around on the planet for about a billion years. They are fungi and are said to be more closely related to animals than to plants. Why is this? They do not produce their own food because, unlike plants, they cannot make chlorophyll. Instead, they get their nutrients by absorbing organic matter from their environment.

From the remarkable to the unbelievable, below are different mushrooms, some even growing on cheeses...!

The strange and different shapes seen at Chelsea 2025 may be the start of some very exclusive and other creations from the mushroom producers in the years to come.

The galvanised wire cages on which the mushrooms were displayed added to the interest of the exhibit rather than detracting from it.

The Little Flower Hut

Many of the stands shown were featured in the Great Pavilion. This little Gem was just one seen, and the kaleidoscope of colour and wildflowers was breathtaking. So many old-fashioned flowers that could leave a person mesmerised at the incredible display, with so many flowers taking my mind back to my childhood.

From wild roses, poppies, and Queen Anne's lace (also known as Wild Carrot), which originated in Southeast Asia and parts of Europe. It is steeped in folklore and is greatly loved by many people who associate it with their home and the countryside. Do not be mistaken, for both giant hogweed and hemlock may be thought to be Queen Anne's Lace; they are not, and both are poisonous plants.

Other flowers included hollyhocks, scabiosa, zinnias, and the charming single-flower miniature dahlias seen opposite.

Other delights included miniature ranunculus bursting with colour, and the scent from these charming gems was like that of the countryside on a gentle summer's evening.

The Magic of Chelsea 2025

Peony Roses

This spectacular display of peony roses was breathtaking, and I said to my husband, 'Am I at a flower show or in a perfumery?' It was a spectacular show of these delightful flowers.

The bumble bees were flocking around the blooms as they opened, and the whole visual purity of the stand was outstanding to see.

The dazzling colours, shape of each flower and the overall presentation were outstanding. We once associated peony roses with a flower that came out briefly in the summertime; they were lovely, but came in white or pink colours.

Now, as you can see in the opposite photograph, there is a gorgeous cream with vibrant gold anthers in the central crown of the flower. Just in one of the open flowers, you can see the cheeky backside of a bee as it forages for nectar!

Another of the delights of this superb day at Chelsea 2025

The Beauty Continues...

The Crescendo...

The peony, first identified in China around 1,000 BCE, has been used in a variety of medicines to treat asthma and headaches and is believed to assist with childbirth.[2]

---

[2] Always check with your health provider before ingesting any medicinal products.

GRASSES

Fabulous grasses, and now with so much colour available in the different types.

From subtle whites to soft pinks, soft greens, and with various leaf formations, they add a dynamic vista to any garden, and they also attract many insects, including butterflies.

The reed-type grass can make a superb visual stopping point with other shorter grasses at its base.

If different grasses are leading to a pond, why not think about planting some Siberian iris to work within the vista.

With many grasses now displayed at the show, it's not easy to include them all.

However, here are just some that were spectacular to see.

My Sweet Pea Story

Have you ever noticed how the atmosphere and surroundings of any room change once a vase of flowers is placed?

Flowers and foliage are living; they are part of the structure of the planet, but they also have other purposes...! They can give off positive energy that allows us to feel it.

Just after my father's passing in 2008, I was at the Chelsea Flower Show and can remember seeing a bank of sweet peas that was tall and wide—a display so large that I have not seen since.

I recall feeling an overwhelming sense of joy, happiness, and connection. I had no idea why this should have happened...! It had been a wonderful day, and as I started to rest and get into bed, I had an immediate vision of my father standing in front of me, looking at the sweet pea display I had seen earlier that day. I think that's why the feeling of connection and belonging came to me as soon as I entered the Great Pavilion and saw the sweet pea display.

Flowers, I believe, are little universal gifts, as well as a way to appreciate the role they play as pollinators.

Sweet peas were first described by a Sicilian monk, Francis Cupani, in his work on the Flora of Sicily, published in 1699. From the first findings, seeds of sweet peas were sent to different parts of the world and have been continually modified into the beautiful flowers we know today.

Perfect Stone...

Nicolas Moreton is a master of his craft, enabling him to transform stone into a creative expression.

From solid, radiating round shapes to expressions of the functioning human body, Nicolas has a deep insight into how the human mind interprets not only shape and form, but also the visualisation of a final creation.

By observing the opposite circular shape and then shifting your gaze to the base, you can see the perfect balance between the two shapes. Not only are the shapes symmetrically placed, but they also become mesmerising and captivating over time.

In the opposite photograph, the spathe of the arum lily takes on a new dimension when viewed back-to-back: the spadix, the inner flower, is sculpted into the familiar shape of the flower we know so well.

From interpretation to creation, beauty has its way of finding and reaching our hearts and minds. Nicolas has a way of transforming ancient rock into a creation of beauty and admiration that we can all enjoy.

The Sculpture of Stone

Through millions of years hidden, the stone used today is honed and sculpted into creative design...

It brings forth the colours of pinks, greys and white sometimes seen, and has more to reveal...

The chiselling away with intent and concentration, for not a chisel or chisel to fault

For if it was, the beauty would result and render naught...

Once, though thought, and finished this form is seen, and yet more work is needed – the beauty revealed: shapes, curves, and angles are seen and none so pure...

For it will last for centuries and allow others to see, and wonder as we do today at the craft to lure...!

Without vision, none would appear. The sculpture of stone is ancient and created by a few.

With fresh ideas and transformations of stone and all so new...

Such splendid control of each chisel strike, and now we see the outcome of the knowledge so keen...

For the heart of the artist is within the work created, and not once do they allow their mind to be abated...

Concentration is the key to working with stone, not allowing the mind to moan...!

Discipline and more are needed to create the image seen, fulfil the role, and allow the emergence of what's in the soul...!

Now, with the image recorded in stone – the artist has fulfilled their role...

The planet reveals its sensational gifts through the talent and skill involved, and yet it is there for us, the viewers, to constantly behold.

The Magic of Chelsea 2025

Begonias in Abundance

Begonias have never lost their popularity, whether as plants sold in nurseries or in flower shops, and the colours and fascination with these timeless flowers continue to this day.

The original begonia is native to Brazil and South America. They thrive in humid environments and shady areas; however, today's commercial varieties have been adapted to meet the demands of the modern marketplace.

In today's varieties, many have dense petal structures that enable them to create large and striking displays in commercial venues, hotel foyers, and at event locations.

As can be seen in these photographs, there is no shortage of colour when it comes to choice.

Framed in the above photograph are the tall larkspur and delphinium plants, which complement the shapes and colours of the begonias. With imagination, many different ideas can become great aspirations and achievements.

Stoned Fruit, Orb Water Features & Containers...

The fruit in the garden featured in the opposite photograph is created from tiny rectangular pieces of stone, horizontally placed and in perfect shape to make these two stone apples and a pear. They are a significant expression of creative talent, yet they possess the quietness of a story being told...

White stone is used in the creation of the opposite orb water feature. It sits in a shallow pool, which creates a feeling of stillness and tranquillity in a restful garden space.

The creative energy in these perfectly formed art presentations is showcased by deep magenta lupins, the green foliage of the lupins, and complementary foliage, which add to the overall inspiring presentation of the display.

With careful thought, many gardens can be transformed into sanctuaries of peace, offering hours of satisfaction and allowing people to appreciate and cherish life's moments.

Plant Biometrics

The Sainsbury Laboratory in Cambridge provided insight into the structure and mechanisms of cell growth in living plants.

I have written many books, and most include human behaviour, which relates, in one aspect, to the flow of hormones and their role in the human body and brain.

We often dismiss the fact that plants, including flowering plants, green plants, and trees, also have hormones. Plants, including trees, will not grow or grow properly if their hormones aren't working correctly.

Hormones are fundamental to all living things.

If you love your plants, when looking at them, remember that your flowering plant is not just a simple structure; like every human, it contains many living components, from tiny molecules to hormones and cellular formations. Your flowers have evolved and developed in shape, form, colour, texture, and various types to attract their pollinators, which perform many roles for the flower, including seed distribution.

Flowers, like human babies, start from a single cell, and similar to the adult human egg, they remain dormant until they meet a male cell—flower fertilisation, which is mainly carried out by insects that visit them.

The process of flower reproduction has developed over millions of years to become what it is today. With new technology, we will learn a great deal more about flowers and grasses, such as wheat and grains. For now, we are fortunate to benefit from nature's evolution and a bit of help from past nurserymen, including my great-uncles, which gives us the privilege of enjoying the flowers and plants of our time.

The Magic of Chelsea 2025

Plant Heritage UK

Plant Heritage is one organisation concerned about the conservation of cultivated plants.

Through care and collection, they are safeguarding almost 1000,000 plants for future generations and the sustainability of the varieties.

Conservation is achieved through the collection of seed pods, as shown below.

Many of the seeds are part of rare collections and not necessarily available on the commercial market.

Above, from pods to development and into maturity.

Within the collection are these rare Clivia seeds. Clivia lily flowers are related to the amaryllis lily, and sometimes they are called the same.

Our plants provide a great variety of our food and therefore need to be protected.

When we care for our plants, we care for our planet!

Flora of South Africa

From magnificent to magical, the Protea stand was on display this year.

Possibly the oldest flower on the planet, it never fails to win admiration from the showgoers. Dating back to at least 300 billion years, the protea is thought to have evolved when Africa was connected to South America, Australia, and New Zealand during the Gondwana period.

The Swedish-born taxonomist named the genus Protea, Carl Linneas, in 1735. The name was inspired by Greek mythology and by the son of Poseidon. This name is thought to reflect the large family of the Proteaceae.

The display in 2025 was beyond the words written in this book, and with hindsight, they do speak for themselves.

Taking The Chelsea Guests into the Story...

To understand the magnitude of the display shown in the Great Pavilion, one must walk around its entire circumference.

To make an impact, different varieties of proteas were grouped. The colours ranged from pinks to deep purples, whites to lemons, and more. There was a sprinkling of blue flowers, which provided a bright contrast and clear separation between each group.

Above, inside the cave, if you look closely, you'll see water dripping into the lake below, a truly remarkable piece of design work.

The design embodies the diversity, adaptability, resilience, and determination of the people who have a vision and wish to showcase the beauty of South Africa to the world.

The Female Face

The smoothness of the finished sculpture is why these two images have been added to the book this year.

The expression captured is one of intrigue and possibly fascination in both faces...

Any delicate chiselling of stone requires patience, precision, and determination, and this is evident in both art exhibits.

Succulents...

Succulents make an excellent addition to an indoor or patio garden. They are easy to care for and can provide gardeners of all ages with hours of quality enjoyment.

The variety of different succulents makes them a good introduction for children to spark an interest in plants, which can then lead to growing easy vegetables, such as carrots. For example, a carrot top can be placed on damp blotting paper in a shallow saucer of water, waiting for the top to sprout green shoots.

Succulents can also be grown on moist blotting paper, just like a carrot.

From carrots to cascading pendants, all are part of the succulent attraction.

Opposite, a beautiful bank of succulents makes an exceptional talking point when added to any garden, terrace or wall feature, as in a vertical or walled garden.

Old-Fashioned Delight...

My mother's family were avid market gardeners and teachers of horticulture and agriculture.

When my parents married, my mother carried a bouquet of white gladioli, which her uncle, a market gardener at Long Crendon, United Kingdom, had made for her in 1945.

These flowers, I'm sure, bring back many memories for many people.

For me, salmon pink was very popular in the sixties here in Australia; each floret was separated, and many florets were fashioned into gladiolus roses. In the sixties and early seventies, many brides and bridesmaids carried these florist-made blooms in their wedding bouquets.

Now that the trend has shifted to hand-tied flower bouquets, I have reservations about these types of bouquets, particularly if the stems are not bound. Bare stems can and do leave stains on beautiful gowns.

There are many ways of constructing wedding bouquets, but it is always the bride's choice that should be considered!

The Magic of Chelsea 2025

Corten Chain Expression & Solid Welded Metal – Creating Art...

In the photograph opposite, the animal-shaped coating appears to be made from strips of Corten steel that are meticulously welded and applied to the shape, representing its fur.

The long-haired cattle seen in these photographs are typical of a breed found in the Scottish Highlands.

These sculptures make an impressive image in the countryside or as a significant landmark.

With so many creative ideas on display this year, there was a surprise around every corner that we took in as we marvelled at the different stands, exhibits, and the creative messages conveyed by the images presented.

From Corten to other metals welded into shapes, all featured expressive motifs, creating a sense of amazement in the eyes of the spectators.

When a Creative Mind is Allowed to have Fun...

On this very same stand, this outstanding artist had other surprises in store...

Upon closer inspection, the thistles and the pelican reveal the intimate details of the sculptures.

With great creative expression, the artist moves from animals to static and the expressive playfulness of music in the creation of the guitar in the photograph below.

With flowers and a butterfly featured in the opposite photograph, it is clear that playtime is in full effect for this creator of magic.

Lots of creative fun, the magic of the day, and the story of the long-haired cattle were all part of such a splendid creation and display seen by thousands as they wandered through an inspiring and fascinating show...

The Magic of Chelsea 2025

DIBLEY'S COLOUR

Dibley's House Plants are a regular exhibit at the Chelsea Flower Show and have won many gold medals. This year's display featured creative colour and superbly presented plants. With an excellent selection of colours and a great range to choose from, the stand had many spectators looking in awe at what was on show.

With finely selected plants and contrasting leaf plants such as begonia and coleus, the spectators were spoilt for choice.

The Streptocarpus gave off its usual splendour of colour with no limitations on its vibrancy.

It wasn't only the vibrant colours that won the Chelsea visitors' hearts, but also the Judges.

From the mellow lavender opposite to vibrant pinks, all were seen in this **GOLD**-winning exhibit.

Agapanthus Flowers

Agapanthus are not truly appreciated for the versatility they offer to the Australian flower arranger.

The floret of the agapanthus flower is ideal for creating headdresses for weddings or for making flower garlands. I have used single-wired florets of agapanthus to make crown-shaped headdresses for brides, and they look amazing.

When our older relatives celebrated a significant wedding anniversary, I used agapanthus as the celebration flower. I arranged about 20 stems of blue agapanthus, cutting the stems to approximately 7.5cm or about 8 inches in length. Then, I secured a half brick of oasis, surrounded by soft chicken wire, to a heavy candlestick. I covered the oasis base with various types of foliage, then inserted the shortened stems of agapanthus to form a ball shape (topiary). Once finished, it was used on a table at the gate to the courtyard and served as a welcome to the many guests who entered the area to join the celebration.

Agapanthus, as cut flowers, have a lot to offer the flower arranger, so please think twice before dismissing them.

Farewell Flowers

This display was a surprise, but it is an inevitable part of life.

Farewell Flowers is a florist that specialises in funeral flowers and tributes.

During my time at university, I spent nearly a year studying people's wishes before they die, and many have specific requests that they want fulfilled.

To make the subject of death and dying a little easier, this flower business offers a range of services.[3]

To add a pun, '...*the design setting was brought to life...*' with mock gravestones and some loose floral designs that were fitting for the display and the message the designers wanted to give to the public audience.

---

[3] www.farewellflowers.co.uk

The casket, made out of cane, added reality to the setting.

A chicken-wire figure sitting on a park bench holding a bunch of flowers adds to the emotion of what is one of life's realities. Alongside the wire figure was a wire-shaped dog. The setting was one of passing, but with careful reflection and letting the time do some of the healing, life can take on a new meaning.

This display was beautiful, which also won **GOLD**, a well-deserved award for a sensitive moment.

The beautiful flower opposite is exceptionally proud to be part of the journey of life.

The Journey...

Life is full of surprises and there's a lot to learn...

From learning to walk and which way to run...!

As time goes on and still more to achieve – for some it's happiness and for some it's to grieve...

Every day has its purpose and time to explore, and there it is – a time to learn more...

From smelling a rose and seeing skies of blue, it's the storms and the feeling, 'Nah...' it's too hard to restore...

Each journey has a challenge, and learning enhances life's purpose and much to achieve.

It's the journey you see, and from a bad experience we want to flee, but quite often, that cannot be...!

For each experience we have, and the difficulties encountered, though all the while it feels no end is in sight...

For the strength that you muster is greater, and with the greater you fight...

The journey continues, and some of life's strength returns; no longer do you accept the trivial concerns...

For life has its purpose, regardless of the journey we travel or the challenges we face; every challenge met is a lesson to be learned.

The journey and purpose we know is to gain the knowledge to sew, which ultimately gives one the time to grow...

LIFE IS A JOURNEY OF LEARNING...

Disbud Chrysanthemums

I love disbud chrysanthemums. Not only do they have a distinguished heritage, but they are worth the money spent on buying just one beautiful specimen.

A fresh disbud will provide weeks of satisfaction when placed singly or incorporated into a modern flower arrangement, such as Sugetsu (distinguished Ikebana) flower design.

Below, the massed pink and white flowers prompt us to hold our breath for a moment as we slowly absorb the work and dedication that have gone into nurturing these magnificent flowers to bring them to this stage of development.

Above, from the soft evoking white to the chartreuse green, they are spectacular blooms.

Chrysanthemums belong to a large family of plants, including Pyrethrum, a natural insecticide. They belong to the Asteraceae family, which includes many daisy-type flowers.

A Magnificent Bloom

From Ancient China and into the twenty-first century, the world has had these fabulous flowers growing from the soil. The emergence of this amazing flower, although not as popular in recent years, is now featured in many bouquets, hand-tied arrangements, and extensive interior displays.

Marble and Stone Carvings

Like so many refined skills, to complete something unique to look at, wonderful to feel, (texture), and when one may think, 'Hmm, I wouldn't mind that in the corner of the courtyard, or down by that maple tree...!' then you may be thinking, this unique piece of work is just what you are looking for...

On our annual trips to Chelsea, I have these thoughts about many of the excellent exhibits we see...

Some exhibits, as seen below, can be exotic, leaving the viewer wondering, while others can be ephemeral, such as the passing of a moment. Each has its own story to tell, and each has required the artist to dedicate many hours of work to achieve the beautiful form presented. Such is the movement of art.

The Magic of Chelsea 2025

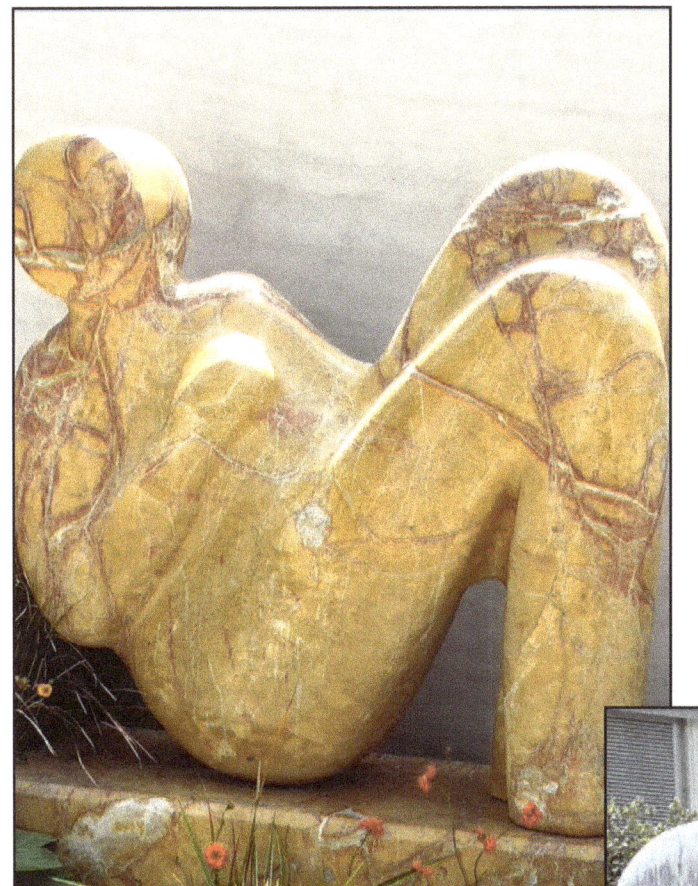

From the suggestive form to the ideas of movement as seen in the opposite interpretation of shape.

With such an understanding of how the human body can become expressive through movement alone, the artist is given scope and time to bring their interpretation to life.

From realism to the way we each think and behave, the artist can take a visual impression and make it into the reality of a stone carving.

The colour of the stone is in itself a remarkable creation of nature, dating back millions, if not billions, of years.

From the reddish-browns of the stone above to the grey and white stippled stone opposite, each has its own character and showcases the beauty it is endowed with.

Inspiration and a chance to craft these remarkable shapes would take time and patience.

Although shaped like the human body, they are not obtrusive and would make an excellent addition to any garden or public setting.

The Magic of Chelsea 2025

Perfect in White

So many beautiful flowers are seen in white. For a reason, they can appeal to our senses of the holy, pure, untouched with simplicity.

For many people, colour can interfere with the pure characteristics of flowers, and therefore, the eternal beauty is lost. However, when white flowers are seen, as in this photograph of full-blown tulips, the magic of the blooms continues…

White flowers can add style, sophistication and design to many interior settings.

Cacti and Succulents

People have used cacti for thousands of years. Most are native to the Americas, with exceptions; some are found in Sri-Lanka. The Incas used them for medicinal purposes, while the Aztecs saw the prickly pear cactus as a symbol of prosperity and fertility.

Cacti have proven over time that they can adapt to arid environments, including the Atacama Desert, one of the driest areas on the planet.

Cacti and succulents have developed thick, fleshy leaves that allow them to store water.

Some of the flowers produced by cacti can be extremely beautiful, with a heavenly scent. The flowers can be exceptionally provocative as they usually appear at night and have a lily-shaped form.

These photographs showcase exceptional specimens of various types that were exhibited at this year's Chelsea Flower Show.

HOSTA PLANTS

Hosta plants can be incredibly striking when viewed as a single houseplant or in mass garden plantings.

Their leaf patterns, striking colours and leaf formation are part of the attraction to the plant.

The Hosta plant originated in China, Korea and Japan. Most were small native plants that grew in shady woodlands, except for Hosta plantaginea, which thrived on the sunny slopes of Korea. This particular plant produces white, lily-shaped flowers that open in the evening, releasing a sweet scent into the evening air.

Such plants are often found in the Korean gardens of monasteries, where monks would tend them.

Some Hosta leaves can reach two feet in size, making a rich and visually striking impact in the garden.

They are ideal for tranquil places and meditation.

Tulips

Many people worldwide adore these stunning flowers. This year, the display by Pheasant Acre showed something different from their usual flowers…! They have turned out every petal of each flower except for these deep-pink ones opposite!

The pink and white tulips below have the treatment of gently easing the open petals through the thumb and index finger, which allows the petals to be seen as focal areas in many floristry presentations.

The easing back of the petals allows the centre of the tulip to be exposed, where you can see the beautiful markings of the flower, the anther, the stigma and the style, all of which are part of the pistil of the flower.

The mass showing of these flowers had an impact and a vibrancy that was all visually absorbing. It was a visual treat that gave the viewer time to stop, look, and become inspired by such marvels created within the world of flowers.

From white to hot pinks and white with a splash of red, all were on display at this year's show.

When I was training in my floristry career, the most prized tulip was the first appearance of the orange-to-apricot Apeldoorn tulip; it is truly a remarkable colour and such a pleasure to use in all arrangements, including wedding bouquets.

As can be seen in the photograph below, there are many colours to choose from and each is spectacular within its own right.

As a bit of a purest myself, when I find a colour that I like, I like to create in just that colour. Singularly coloured arrangements give impact, taste, and a sense of sophistication, as well as a touch of interior design, and are indeed a feature of many garden displays…

The Magic of Chelsea 2025

The Seed of Obsession...

With many concerns about the planet and its future, many people and countries are taking the well-being and future into their own hands to ensure the preservation of many plants. Orchids are just one flower that has people concerned.

Orchid societies are just one area of conservation for this much-loved and admired plant in so many countries.

Not only does the range offer a fabulous range of colours, but the shapes and configuration of the petal formation can leave one awe-struck.

With so many excellent specimens on display at this year's show, it was challenging to include them all. It is, however, thanks to the courtesy of the many displays shown at this year's show, that we can bring this information to you.

It is almost from the archives of the orchid hunters that some of these beautiful and sometimes rare plants can survive.

When you examine the complex shapes, all adapted to their local climate and the conditions in which they lived, it reveals the plant's versatility and the determination encoded in its DNA to survive.

Equally so is the slipper orchid, or Paphiopedium, seen here above or opposite.[4]

---

[4] RHS Chelsea 2025: Orchids, Conservation & Global Collaboration

The Magic of Chelsea 2025

Small Gardens for Unique Spaces...

A space to call our own is essential when life is busy and there is little time to 'sit!'

The garden space opposite offers a serene retreat and a moment of peace amidst a busy lifestyle.

Corten steel containers can provide quick yet effective garden solutions in small spaces. Beams should be professionally installed to create a design, but if a hanging chair isn't included, a back wall or fence is all that's needed.

Opposite, green-painted metal boxes, a concrete garden bench, the back wall and some tasteful cushions allow this design to flow.

Quiet summer nights can be a welcome treat after a busy workday. Soft flower plants, some ornamental grasses, and the small white stones add to the ambience of the setting.

Again, a time to stop and let the world go by...

If cost is a factor and you love to dabble in the garden but only have a small space, have you considered building a potting shed and garden bench out of found wood?

The opposite workspace may help you relax, feel the earth between your fingers, and allow some special time for planting.

Life is made up of moments, and it's those special, quiet moments that allow us, each and individually, to reconnect with nature and the reason we love to do the things we do.

The opposite small garden demonstrates how effective flat pieces of slate or rock can be used to create different features, plains, and add depth to a small space.

With this idea, a water feature could be added to enhance the scene, allowing the setting to have movement not only from the running or bubbling water and the rustling of the leaves, but also from the visual impact of the space.

Nostalgia is a wonderful sentiment, and here we have the red phone box, which is so reminiscent of times gone by!

With a plethora of white and blue flowers, planted also on the floor of the box, the feeling evoked is one of great admiration and fond memories for many people.

The traditional summer flowers used may evoke many memories of childhood, a walk in the park on a late summer afternoon, or of old family gardens.

Emotions were captured here in a single moment of creative expression.

For those with an old shed in the back garden, this creative use of colour and imagination brings excitement and a sense of wonder to a garden space.

Also considered are the insect hotels seen on the walls, which are painted in happy colours.

With quiet respect, this idea would make an excellent learning environment for our little people who are intrigued by insect behaviour.

Gently planted old favourites, such as nasturtium, also add to the delight of the stand.

Opposite, it is the sophistication of the moment, with sharp square angles that show how shape can be delightful when created with taste and awareness.

Subtle colours, combined with dense plantings, also make this a showstopper.

The wooden lounge and bolster back cushion, although they have been in fashion for a long time, offer practical comfort when viewed in this light.

On early spring mornings, with a cup of coffee in your hand, it would be nice to take a moment before the rush of the day begins…!

Opposite, the scene hanging from the back wall adds a nice dimension to a rather Mexican-feeling display.

The tubs of herbs and the large potted lavender bush waft a scent through the air, creating a sense of seclusion. It would be an ideal spot, facing a field or forested land, to have a bath or Jacuzzi with gently planted herbs in the garden pavement or floor setting.

Peace, tranquillity and a sense of oneness will allow relaxation to happen.

Oriental Lilies

Fabulous blooms, amazing colours, and natural, heavenly perfumes, all in one flower…!

As technology becomes more refined, natural perfumes may be synthesised to mimic these wonderful and heavenly scents.

Having done a great deal of research into food and drink additives for my books, Devils In Our Food, Editions One and Two, and because of the advancement in technology, many natural foods, flavours, tastes, appearance and other attributes that natural food have are now mimicked to look real, but many are fake.

The amazing perfume of these fabulous flowers may also be replicated in the future. However, for the moment, let us all enjoy these heavenly-scented blooms in our homes and in our lives.

Grandness and elegance in one single viewing!

The Oriental Lily, also known as the Star Gazer lily, was the first of its kind to be successful and possibly the most successful lily to date. In 1974, Dr Leslie Woodriff succeeded in creating a hardy, perfumed specimen of the flower.

The Oriental lily is believed to have originated in Asia, specifically in Japan and China.

Lilies have been depicted in cartouche symbols, paintings, or used in symbolism since approximately 1,500 BCE.

The story of this amazing lily is fascinating. Before World War II, a farmer named Hirotaka Uchida and his son nurtured and developed the original lily in Japan for its hardiness and durability. After the war, the lily was brought to America, where it was further developed into the wonderful blooms we see today.

The Magic of Chelsea 2025

Clematis Wonder...

A pathway of wonder as you walk along this magical journey into the world of Clematis.

With a delicate perfume and soft, gentle petals, this flower offers its beauty to share...

So many blooms in absolute abundance, with the gentle anthers and markings of each flower a little different.

With so many people wanting to see this splendid showing, we were fortunate to have found a space within the crowd, which seemed as though it was all meant to be.

It was a private moment for the flower and the spectator to spend quietly together, just for that moment in time...!

And so, for a short time only, we can relish this mass beauty of colour and form!

From pinks, to purples, whites and lavenders, they were all gleaming and wanting to be seen.

When nature gives us such beauty and so many pleasures, it is time to stop, look, enjoy and mellow in the moment at what is before us.

Marvelling at this creation and how its colours are so perfect is a pleasure for the brain and mind to experience.

My mother would often say, '*Look into the face of the flower...*'

Opposite is the face of the flower she would speak of.

How perfect a creation to see, so feminine and delicate, if I were to go into one of my roles when I'm writing a children's book, I would see tiny fairies, dancing, sitting, wondering and possibly thinking of the next piece of mischief they could create...

It all depends on how we interpret these beautiful images.

The Magic of Chelsea 2025

The Art of Seeing...

'Look Deeply into the Face of the Flower,' my mother said.

Wild & Free – All Created from Found Wood...

Human ingenuity continually seeks new ways to create something unique. In this age of awareness and the last fifty years' surge in consumerism, people are now exploring alternative methods to craft from found or recycled objects.

These decorative garden creations, through weathering, are strong and lend themselves to many garden features. From wild horses to hares of the meadow, each shows its personality and character from the effective form of movement in the wood creation.

Who could deny the realistic features of this beast of the wild... A bear roaming and possibly observing what is happening in his neighbourhood...

A garden built or modelled with this creature in mind would be different and incredibly striking.

The realistic features of the animals created take into account the

muscular strength of the animals in their visual movement. Although static, they are remarkable, considering every piece of wood is different in size, colour, and texture.

If you look carefully at the eagle, you will see there is an eel or snake in its beak.

From the wildness of the creature evoked and the precision of the mastery in controlling the materials to create this exhibit, it becomes an exciting exhibit to see.

From the wide span of the wings seen in the eagle's wings, to the hares bounding in a meadow. Speed, movement, and telling the true story of the animals and how they live in their habitats make this stand interesting to see.

Having said that, time is needed to absorb the intricate details of the animals in the scenes.

Like so many forms of art, time is taken and forward thinking is needed before the creation comes into being…

Arisaema Sikokianum

Or the Japanese Cobra lily, as it is also known.

It is different and interesting to look at. It would make a spectacular plant for a feature display in the home or be featured in a mass display for either corporate or hotel foyers.

They are seasonal plants coming out in the springtime. In mid-to-late autumn, they have striking red berries. A further asset of the plant is its divided leaves, which can have a cream to silver splash of colour.

In the opposite photograph, a different variation of the Cobra lily, known as the Japanese Dominatrix Pulpit lily.

They can be both weird and fascinating to people who have not seen them before. Still, they are highly admired by professional orchid collectors and nurserymen who appreciate the diverse range of plant varieties.

Their colours are not vibrant but subtle and sometimes mottled, ranging from all tones, tints, and shades of greens, deep brownish to reds and slight variations of these colours in between…!

The Magic of Chelsea 2025

Jacques Amand

With so many excellent colours always featured on the Jacques Amand stand, winning **GOLD** is well deserved.

Exotic, stunning colours and flowers shown each year leave the florist or flower lover with the desire to cut, arrange and enjoy…!

Such vivid contrasts and so many different varieties, and yet, they are there waiting for us to look, linger and think…!

The beautiful specimen of a lily captured this year in the opposite photograph almost looks like the flower has been painted in watercolour; it is so perfect.

From magical shapes, textures and formations, the Jacques Amand stand captures one's imagination.

The Magic of Chelsea 2025

Looking at every flower in the above photograph leaves no doubt as to the grandness of each flower as it flaunts itself in the bid to be noticed and its picture taken.

The extraordinary individuality of each flower draws you in, and the delight of the exhibit is breathtaking.

The richness of the green leaves in the lower part of the photograph, moving visually upwards to the yellows and salmon pink of the Kniphofia flowers, reaching and blending into the lilac, white, and pink allium, creates an almost Rembrandt-like collection of colours within the picture.

Feature a Circle...

It isn't easy to imagine life without circles... Just think of the sun, the moon, a dinner plate, a ball wouldn't bounce if it weren't round and shaped like a circle...

Many pieces of fruit are round in shape, such as apples, oranges, peaches, and plums, as well as other natural objects that are shaped like a circle.

It isn't often that we see the circle as an embellishment in a garden, and what a magical and mesmerising shape it is when we pause and gaze at it!

A circle has no break, which is why, when we buy flowers, a wreath for a loved one or someone who has passed away is often crafted in a circle. This is an ancient belief, but the tradition of gifting flower wreaths at funerals continues.

A wreath, without a gap, prevents the spirit of the deceased from returning and rising from the ground. The unbroken circle is a superstition meant to keep any evil spirit or energy securely within the grave or where the living and their superstitions want it to stay.

Having said that, incorporating a circle as a garden feature can be visually relaxing and serve as a focal point of interest.

The Magic of Chelsea 2025

Tonal Value & Shape
OF COLOUR WITH CONTRASTING SCULPTURED FRUIT

Shape is an integral part of everything in everyday life. From the bed you sleep in to the dress or trousers worn, to the armchairs or the saucepan on the stove, each and everything has shape.

In the opposite photographs, it is the shape of a blue apple and a bronze pear that draws the visual gaze, and then we look at the soft planting used, which enhances the shape of the fruit.

The shape in the opposite photograph is also what is making the exhibits distinctive and appealing. The shape of the shell could be that of a garden snail or a seashell, but it is the solid, beautiful curve of the shape, combined with the bronze colour, that makes it interesting to look at.

Texture also plays a significant role in this tasteful exhibit, from the greys of the apple seen in the distance, the grey of the acorn, and the pinnacles of the Reuleaux triangles, which feature aqua and lattice.

Different Outside Gardens for Different Reasons –

British Red Cross...

The British Red Cross garden was a showpiece and a delight to see.

The theme is *'Here for Humanity'*. The Garden was a contemporary interpretation of an alpine garden, with traditional associations and trough displays, as seen in the photograph opposite.

Specimen trees, such as Arolla pines, add height and distinction, complementing the calming effect of the water flowing against the solid stone and its hexagonal shape.

From the height of the trees, leading the viewer to the continued hexagonal shapes in the pathway, and the gentle planting of delicate herbs, this leaves an impression of care and thoughtfulness.

It is the combination of love, care and persistence that shows us that the British Red Cross is: *'Here for Humanity.'*

Different Gardens for Different Reasons...

From stunning architectural creations to the practicality of the design.

'Save for a Rainy Day,' Garden was inspiring, both in the building's construction and in the rock placements, along with the plantings, which evoke the South of France or Northern Spain.

From lovely garden flowers used in plantings in crevices and between rocks, a magical atmosphere is created in these spaces.

Precious moments of contemplation would be complete moments of pleasure in such a setting.

A garden designed to withstand changing weather conditions, while still allowing people to enjoy their gardens, can be achieved with hardy plants and drought-resistant trees. This approach maintains the human desire to love and care for their gardens.

Different Gardens for Different Reasons – The Avanade Intelligent Garden

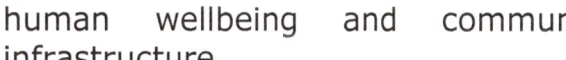

An urban forest garden designed to stimulate the human senses.

With plantings of hardy urban trees that help filter the air and reduce pollution, trees also help keep the air cooler in rising temperatures, support wildlife, and contribute to overall human wellbeing and community infrastructure.

The garden features productive fruit-bearing trees and a diverse array of edible plants.

This garden utilises technology to an extreme degree. With a web-based app, we can 'speak to the trees' and learn how to care for and maintain them for maximum health.

Other features include a pavilion built from clad-based wood pulp panels infused with mycelium (an essential element in healthy root-like structures supporting all forms of plant growth).

Different Gardens for Different Reasons – Children with Cancer UK 'A Place to Be...'

Children love to play and have fun. It is with the aspiration of a parent that I find this garden delightful.

When a parent sees their child gravely ill, all they want is for their child to recover, be well and have the ability to live their life to its fullest potential.

A garden that embraces nature, where children can escape from the rigorous routine of their treatment and find some play time or a time to wonder and love the moments.

We have had a child diagnosed with type 1 diabetes, and watching a healthy child's health rapidly decline is heartbreaking for any parent. When we see our child enjoying the space, it brings happiness to the heart. The plants have been chosen for their colour, scent and movement. It also offers children a short monorail ride and a meandering path of abundant plantings, which leads to a quiet, peaceful sanctuary—a lovely place for any child to enjoy.

The 'O' Shape

For many of us, our garden is our sanctuary. A place where you hope you will not be disturbed, a place where you enjoy digging in the earth and a time that belongs to just you…

These may be wishful words for many, but if by chance, there is a circle in the garden, it can make even a brief time spent a time of restoring and grounding.

From static round shapes or symbols, to running water as in the opposite photograph, round shapes have this power, and why is this?

On the scientific side of the answer, 'Our brains can process a circle shape easily and quickly. This process does not

challenge the brain, and this is why looking at a circle promotes relaxation and calmness. On the ethereal side, circles allow us to see a sense of unity, harmony and infinity. A circle also symbolises completeness and symmetry, creating a feeling of balance and togetherness. They may also instil the thought that we are indeed part of something greater than ourselves, and give the feeling of inclusivity.

There may be many health benefits to installing or having an 'O' shape in the garden…!

Spectacular Zantedeschai Plants & More...

Pretty as Paint...

These perfect little gems of flowers are wonderful as potted plants or seen growing in the garden.

Having said that, they are magical flowers used in commercial floristry, either in traditional or modern flower arrangements, or as bridal flowers in wedding bouquets.

There is a tiny bridal Zantedeschia that looks stunning in bridal bouquets; it is the shape of the flower that enhances the elegance of the bouquet.

The colours are always bright, and have a freshness and crispness not always seen in flowers.

The leaves can also make a key statement when used in the focal area of the flower arrangements and design, or when cut down, they can add to the wedding bouquet.

If Zantedeschia leaves are used in any form of design, ensure they are crisp.

Soft leaves will not firm up; they will only droop more without water.

The Magic of Chelsea 2025

The Flowers We See Today...

Often missed, the flowers we see today...
Some with a single petal and some with a multitude to play...!

For millions of years, this adaptation has taken place, when only they can find their own personal space...

For it is their survival that plays an important part, for none would be here if they didn't have a start...!

Such wonders have taken place, and none would know how much, for such is the nature in the world's evolution, they say...

Colours of plenty and none the same, goodness, 'what is their name...?'

Some so long and difficult to say, such as Arisaema sikokianum
And, you ask, 'what was that...?'

For that is the nature of the plants we see, some so different, and it's difficult to explain... for they are all part of the major plan...

For each has its role and job to do, for often with mining and felling of trees, many species are now on their knees –

It's time to take a second look, for without flowers growing in healthy habitats and allowed to survive...

The people and new generations will struggle, and the future looks grim...!

Now is the time; we know the risks involved. With forward thought, so many problems can be solved...

Every person has their role to play, so easy it is, and none can say...!

Let's take responsibility and share the work and vigilance needed...
For the rewards are so great, we cannot be heeded...!

And so the journey begins, the flowers we know and want to grow...

From the single spathe blooms and the rose with petals to share, all of which need our care...!

If we don't act, the flowers we see today will be no longer....

That is not a legacy to leave for in our hearts; we must be stronger...

Nature's Offering & so Much More...

In our book, The Magic of Chelsea (2024), we included a brief article on these fascinating trees.

It was charming to see this stand represented again at this year's show.

In the photograph below, and to the left, the tree branches are intertwined to create a unique and distinct effect.

It suggests that many single trees were planted and allowed to grow to a certain height, then trained into the shapes we see today.

It would take many years of dedication and work to create these wonderful and decorative plants.

They are indeed a pleasure to look at and would be ideal in large hotel foyers or as a talking point at various venues.

Looming Threat – The Colorado Beetle...

The Colorado Beetle looks harmless enough, but in both the United Kingdom and Australia, it poses a threat to popular crops, such as potatoes and tomatoes.

It devours the leaves of these crops, which also include eggplant, pepper or any plants within the nightshade family.

The Colorado Beetle is easily recognisable due to its brightly coloured body, featuring yellow, red, and black stripes.

The larvae are also easily recognisable because of the orange-pink colour.

They have a 9-segmented abdomen, can measure up to 15mm and have a black head.

Due to their voracious eating habits, they can easily destroy crops if not controlled or eliminated. Vigilance is needed to stop this pest in its tracks, so please be on the lookout; this beetle is not a friend or a cute insect but a destroyer of food.

The weather was lovely without a cloud in the sky, so different to last year, it was a truly magical day...

A Fantastic 2025 Chelsea

Inspiration from an Empty Space...

Enterprising ventures keep a country's economy moving forward.

On our quick trip to Devon after our day out at Chelsea, it was a wonderful surprise to see the Catkin Blooms coffee shop, florist, nursery and gift shop open in Winkleigh, Devon. At our last visit in 2024, the space was an empty garage, but now it is a thriving community hub.

The café serves up delicious homemade cakes and food, and has excellent coffee.

It is family- and dog-friendly, offering a variety of meetings and workshops.

All the flowers on sale are grown locally and delivered to the shop on the day they are picked, resulting in a minimal carbon footprint with these blooms.

In the photograph below, with such a fabulous asset for the community, it isn't any wonder these delightful ladies stop from their gardening and have morning tea...!

There is an excellent range of locally made gifts on display and at affordable prices.

If 'time out' is all that is needed, then you can sit quietly and enjoy a favourite cuppa!

The coffee shop, florist and gift store sit at the 'T' Junction of this delightful Devonshire village.

With friendly people, delightful cakes and savouries, fantastic coffee, what else could a traveller ask for...?

Beautiful Devon, gorgeous countryside, and such precious moments on our journey.

Children's artwork was a feature of the front counter where our coffee was served.

All in all, a wonderful, friendly experience while on our way back to Heathrow for the flight back to Australia.

My words to you...

Life is what you make it...!

We can't control all of the aspects of our lives, but we can learn from our experiences.

I first trained as a florist in London during the 1960s, and it was an interesting fact that I identified: 'Why do people buy flowers?' This one question led me to nine years of study at the University of Canberra and the Canberra School of Art in Australia, where I sub-majored in 20th-century art history and sculpting. I have also graduated from the university with a degree in teaching, complemented by a major in psychology.

Psychology is essentially the study of how we each behave in various situations. All behaviour is prompted by our perception and understanding of the circumstances we encounter. Once perceived, the message is relayed through the body's electrical system, allowing it to be sent to the brain. The brain then releases different hormones, which enable our muscles to move, and we respond accordingly.

This book, The Magic of Chelsea, focuses on relaxation and enjoyment for the reader. It encourages savouring and loving every moment on each page. Turning the pages helps you to mellow and easily absorb the information, which naturally promotes relaxation. In turn, your brain and body respond positively. Your muscles relax, and the enjoyment of the photographs takes you on a visual journey. The brief descriptions support your understanding of each exhibit.

My foundation in becoming a florist comes from an extensive five-year training program. Although it was challenging at the time, it provided me with the deep knowledge necessary for my articles. Similarly, nine years of university education have helped me to develop my writing skills.

I am thankful to all the teachers I have had throughout my life. I have also learnt a lot from my learning experiences, both good and bad, and gained more from the challenging and humiliating ones than I possibly could have from continuous positive outcomes. From the difficult times in life, I have learnt resilience and determination, and every moment I have is a moment to use to create something beneficial and positive for those I love or to work on a book.

Christine

The Magic of Chelsea 2025

LIFE SKILLS EDUCATION ASSOCIATION

ONLINE COURSES FOR FAMILIES, TEENS, ADULTS, COMMUNITY GROUPS, INCLUDING SCHOOLS, COMMERCIAL AND GOVERNMENT

The Life Skills Education Association has been established because many young people and adults struggle to cope with the demands of living in a highly competitive and technologically advanced age.

Life skills education is often missing in mainstream education, which leaves many children, teens and adults vulnerable to being abused, used or misled. Life skills education provides the child, teen, or adult with the information that builds in the individual's memory to act accordingly when they find themselves in trouble.

Life skills enable a person to think forward and take proactive actions. In many instances, we may learn after the incident has taken place and have the common thought, 'I wouldn't do that again…' or 'I wish I had known that sooner…!' This is a reactive learning approach and is the standard way of learning after being hurt, either physically or emotionally.

We now have the opportunity, thanks to technology and online education, to support our younger people, including teens and adults, in building their life skills. Our online education can also help people who face numerous challenges, including managing stress, children and teens navigating puberty, and many other real-life situations.

Our books on the following pages will give you an idea of the number of topics covered, some of which have been converted into online packages.

Please get in touch with us by email: admin@fullpotentialtraining.com.au for more information.

Other Books
Available Online & THROUGH LEADING BOOK OUTLETS

www.how2books.com.au

The book, 'How To Create Easy Wedding Bouquets,' introduces you to many techniques in wedding bouquet construction, the different methods used to wire various flowers and leaves, how to tape ribbon onto the wedding bouquet handle, how to make a corsage, hand-tied bouquets, buttonhole, and other industry skills that will start you on a floristry career.

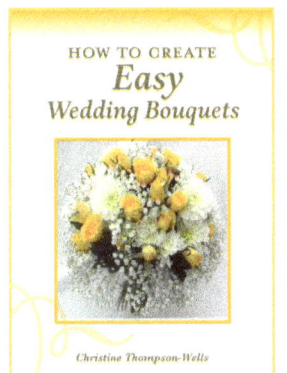

Our education company, Full Potential Education & Training, was established to help individuals develop skills in the floristry industry. The course is a CPD-accredited 20-week online program in commercial floristry and wedding bouquet making. It aims to support individuals who want to start their own business or pursue a trade career in floristry. To purchase this book, please visit www.how2books.com.au.

'How To Create Easy Flower Arrangements' introduces floral art and commercial floristry in flower arranging. The book is designed to help individuals who want to learn flower arranging and construction techniques, providing the foundational knowledge necessary for those who wish to pursue a career in the floristry industry.

It will also help people who want to learn flower arranging for enjoyment and gifting, as well as creating arrangements for special occasions. To buy this book, please visit www.how2books.com.au.

The Magic of Chelsea, 2022, includes information about the Chelsea Flower Show. It features over 250 photographs and more than 125 pages of detailed content about the show, its exhibitors, flower stands, displays, and other helpful information, including some contact details for stand exhibitors. To buy this book, visit www.how2books.com.au.

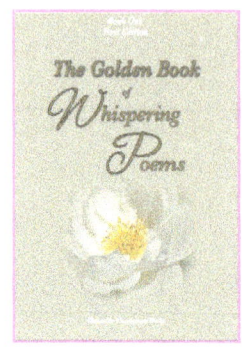

Because we love the books we create and poetry is a significant part of our work, we couldn't resist including this collection of different poems. To buy this book, please visit www.how2books.com.au.

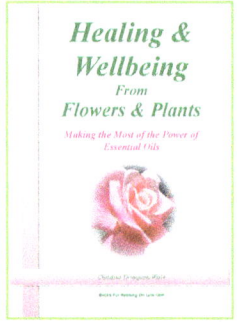

Without plants, we would not be able to survive. As all flower lovers know, many plants and trees are under threat! Plants not only help to keep our planet and wildlife healthy, but they also contribute to our human well-being.

This book outlines the benefits of using herbs in our everyday lives. It is colourful and gives a breakdown of herb uses. To purchase this book, please go to www.how2books.com.au.

The Magic of Chelsea, 2023, features comprehensive information about the Chelsea Flower Show. It includes over 250 photographs and more than 125 pages of detailed content about the event, its exhibitors, flower stands, displays, and other helpful information, including some contact details for stand exhibits. To buy this book, visit www.how2books.com.au.

The Magic of Chelsea, 2024, features a wide range of photographs that take you on a journey through the entire magical show.

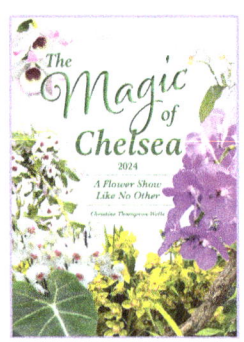

With so many different displays and amazing exhibits, it's not easy to cover everything we saw, and this remains true for each year we attend. Many talented and extraordinary individuals bring their products to the annual event, having worked hard throughout the year to showcase new and exciting items, including plants, sculptures, and more. To buy this book, visit www.how2books.com.au.

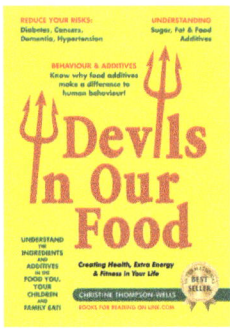

There are many concerns about the quality of food currently consumed by our global population. With the increasing number of health issues and illnesses scientifically linked to food additives, this book highlights the 'nasties' in the global food supply chain. Now endorsed by many doctors, this book will guide you on discovering and understanding how contaminated foods affect your well-being and good health. To purchase this book, please visit www.how2books.com.au.

With so many questions about what to eat, we have researched and published Devil Free Recipes. These recipes take you on a journey into new ways of preparing quality, healthy food full of natural nutrition that sustains the body and brain's performance, boosts sustainable energy levels, and restores the natural taste of food to your taste buds. To buy this book, please visit www.how2books.com.au

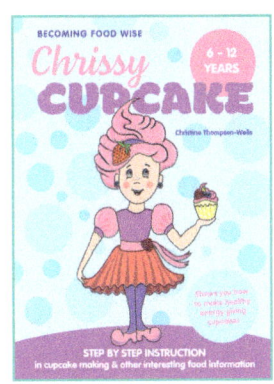

When children are between 6 and 7 years old, or even earlier, they often start to show an interest in how their food is prepared and generally want to help in the kitchen.

One of the areas often overlooked is the safety a child needs to know before they start making their tasty treat, their first cupcake. Chrissy Cupcake guides the child through the first steps, including identifying cooking and cake utensils, staying safe in the kitchen, and the correct way to work with knives and other utensils. To buy this book, please visit www.how2books.com.au

General Reading

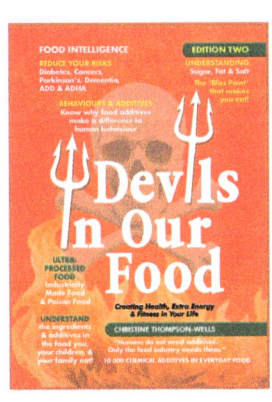

Devils in Our Food, 2nd Edition, is a recent release that highlights the increasing number of food and drink additives entering the global food supply chain, with up to 15,000 additives now present.

Everyday foods, such as bread and biscuits, are now being added without either consumer consent or the correct food information being entered into the food ingredient panel of the product. Many soft drinks, including fresh juices, can also be manufactured. To buy this book, please visit www.how2books.com.au

Age is a privilege that should be cherished. However, as the body ages, it needs to be worked to stay healthy, pliable and resilient. Regular, yet passive, exercise is a way to build muscle tone and stay fit.

Science now shows that exercise benefits not only the body but also the brain. Regular physical activity helps you think more clearly, be more assertive, and develop a range of interests as you age. Exercises can be done in the quiet of your home, sitting on a chair or using the end of a bed for balance. To buy this book, please visit www.how2books.com.au.

Menopause doesn't only start when a woman is in her fifties. Some younger women, in their twenties, may go into menopause. Menopause is a sign that the body is changing. In older women, it is a sign that the child-bearing years are over. Each woman's experience of menopause is different; therefore, every woman's story is different. There is no 'one-size-fits-all' solution for the naturally changing conditions. This book helps identify some of the changes and guides how to manage them. To buy this book, please visit www.how2books.com.au

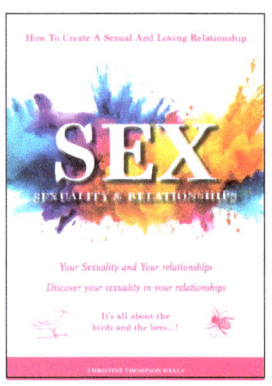

With respect and admiration for the human body's remarkable functions during various experiences. The book examines the changing chemistry of the biological and physiological processes during different experiences in human relationships.

Understanding how we each react during different and intimate moments in our lives helps us reach certain levels of understanding and acceptance that we are all different, and that each relationship works in its own way. Respect for oneself and others is the ultimate knowledge within all successful relationships. Having said that, many variables are interacting continuously in all relationships. To buy this book, please visit www.how2books.com.au.

Many young people are sensitive to the physical changes that occur during puberty. New research has found that puberty may start as early as six years old; geographic locations may influence this, but awareness remains essential. Each young person is different and will follow their own body's timetable. To buy this book, please visit www.how2books.com.au.

Our series of 'Changes' books is designed for individual, group, or family participation. Each of the four 'Changes' books features an engaging six-chapter story at the start. These stories depict children from diverse parts of the world, showcasing how they form friendships and encounter various experiences as they transition from childhood to adulthood. The second half of the book is a workbook that can be used for self-reading, working with the family or in one-to-one discussion.

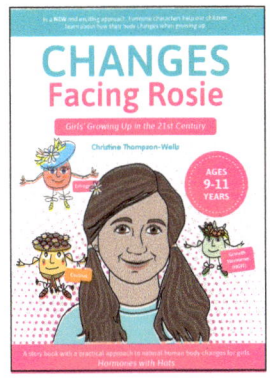

In this series, there are separate books for boys and girls. Each is written with the knowledge of being age-appropriate, targeting readers aged 9 to 11 years and 11 to 14 years. To buy this book, please visit www.how2books.com.au.

From the ages of 11 to 14, the books maintain the same format, featuring an exciting six-chapter adventure at the start. The second part of the book allows the young person to read alone, work in a group, or collaborate with family members.

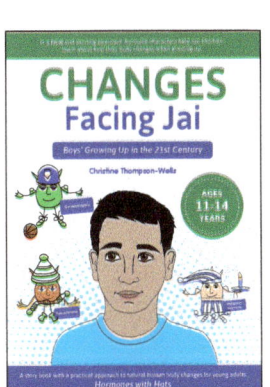

With books designed to build life skills, such as our puberty awareness books, working with sensitivity supports the child during their period of change.

Each of us experiences change, and some of these are key to growing and maturing into adulthood. Recognising that not only the body is changing but also the brain, the more knowledge shared, the safer the young person will be.

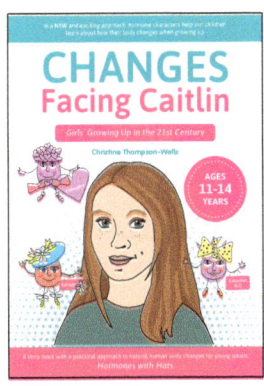

Note: Although the human brain develops around the age of 7, it does not fully mature until a young person is approximately 25 years old. By then, the neuron pathways are connected, and the individual gains a deeper understanding of their world, responsibilities, and commitments to reality. To buy any of these books, please visit www.how2books.com.au

Only a few of our books are mentioned here; there are more Life Skill books available on our website: http://www.how2books.com.au

This book is brought to you from the publishers of:

ISBN: 978-1-7642897-0-2

www.ingramcontent.com/pod-product-compliance
Lightning Source LLC
Chambersburg PA
CBHW061401070526
44583CB00026B/3232